Mini Artist
Printing

Toby Reynolds

WINDMILL
BOOKS™
New York

Published in 2015 by Windmill Books, An Imprint of Rosen Publishing
29 East 21st Street, New York, NY 10010

Editor for Windmill: Joshua Shadowens

Photo Credits: Illustrations by Fiona Gowen; Images on pages 2 and 3 © fotolia.com.

Library of Congress Cataloging-in-Publication Data

Reynolds, Toby, author.
 Printing / by Toby Reynolds.
     pages cm. — (Mini artist)
 Includes index.
 ISBN 978-1-4777-9127-1 (library binding) — ISBN 978-1-4777-9128-8 (pbk.) —
ISBN 978-1-4777-9129-5 (6-pack)
 1. Handicraft—Juvenile literature. I. Title.
 TT160.R434 2015
 745.5—dc23
                                    2014001203

Manufactured in the United States of America

CPSIA Compliance Information: Batch #WS14WM: For Further Information contact Windmill Books, New York, New York at 1-866-478-0556

Mini Artist **Printing**

Contents

4

Getting Started

The projects in this book use lots of art **materials** that you will already have at home. Any missing materials can be found in an art supply store.

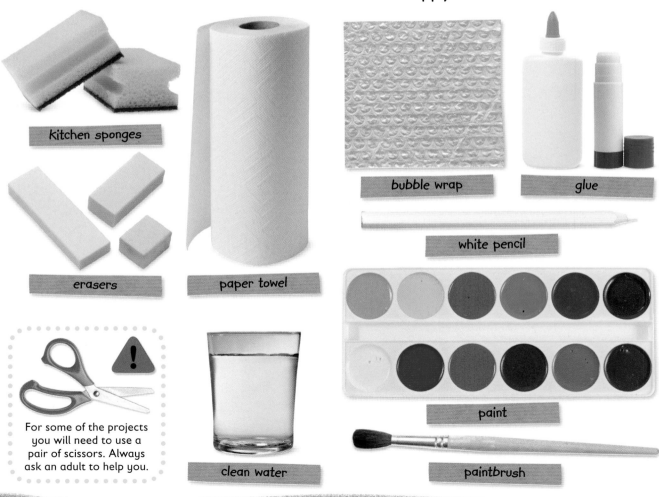

kitchen sponges

bubble wrap

glue

erasers

white pencil

paper towel

paint

For some of the projects you will need to use a pair of scissors. Always ask an adult to help you.

clean water

paintbrush

string

leaves

felt-tip pens

Handy Hint

parsnip

potato

leek

You can create many shapes and **patterns** with different types of vegetables. Experiment with whatever you can find.

Here is a selection of the paper you will need to complete all the printing projects.

Swirly Butterfly

To make these butterflies, you need a felt-tip pen, colored paper, paints, water and a brush.

1 Start by taking a piece of colored craft paper. Fold the paper in half to form a crease, then open it back up.

2 Take your paints and a brush and add a few dots of colored paint on one side of the paper.

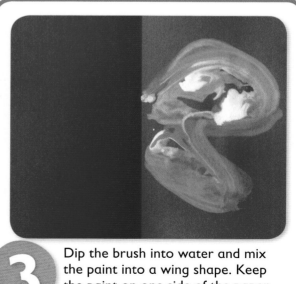

3 Dip the brush into water and mix the paint into a wing shape. Keep the paint on one side of the paper.

4 While the paint is wet, fold the paper and press down firmly. Open up the paper to see your butterfly!

5 Ask an adult to cut out the shape of the butterfly. You can then glue this onto a large white piece of paper.

6 To finish your picture use a black felt-tip pen to draw the body and two **antennae** onto the butterfly.

Potato Paper

To make this pretty patterned picture, you will need paints, paper and some potatoes.

1 Choose a medium-sized potato. Make sure it is clean by washing it in water. Dry it with paper towels.

2 Ask an adult to cut the potato in half. The two pieces of potato will become your two stamps.

3 Take one stamp and place it flat side down into some orange paint. Place the other stamp into some red paint.

4 Take the orange stamp and carefully press it paint side down onto the top left hand corner of the paper.

5 Now take the other stamp and print next to the first. Do this again until you have filled the whole paper.

6 Make two more stamps with a small potato and print different colors into the original circles.

Spongy Fish

To make this fish picture, you will need a kitchen sponge, blue paper, paints, a pen and scissors.

1 Use a black felt-tip pen to draw the basic **outline** of a fish onto the base of a clean kitchen sponge.

2 Now you can ask an adult to cut the sponge into the shape of your fish. This will become your stamp.

3 Gently dip the stamp into some white paint. Don't press hard as you don't need much paint on the stamp.

4 Take the stamp and place it onto the blue paper. Don't press down hard on the stamp or it will get messy.

5 Now you can put some more white paint onto the stamp and print lots more fish all over the paper.

6 To finish your picture, use a small circle of sponge to print some bubbles using blue paint.

Leafy Bookmark

It is fun to make these leafy bookmarks. You will need leaves, cardboard, scissors and paints.

1 Collect a small selection of leaves. It is a good idea to have leaves of different sizes and shapes.

2 Take some thin cardboard and cut it into long rectangles. These are your bookmarks ready to decorate.

3 Brush some bright paint onto the underside of a leaf. This is the side of the leaf with ridges and veins on it.

4 Put the leaf paint-side down onto the cardboard. Gently press the leaf so all of it touches the bookmark.

5 Repeat this several times. You can add more paint onto the leaf before pressing it down again.

6 Try experimenting with different paint colors and leaf shapes to make lots of bookmarks.

Handy Octopus

All you need to create this octopus is some blue paper, paints and a black felt-tip pen.

1 Choose a color for your octopus. Paint it over the palm of your hand and press down on some blue paper.

2 Wash the paint off and then paint your other hand. Press it down to make this octopus shape.

3 When the paint has dried you can use white paint and your fingers to print eyes onto the octopus.

4 When the white paint has dried, use a black felt-tip pen to make a smile. Add some black circles in the eyes.

5 Decorate your octopus by dipping your fingertip in yellow paint and dabbing spots on the tentacles.

6 To finish the picture, you could add a few fingerprint fish and then paint some green seaweed.

Friendly Bug

To make this fun caterpillar, you will need a kitchen sponge, scissors, paints and a felt-tip pen.

1 Use a black felt-tip pen to draw a big circle and a small circle onto the the base of a clean kitchen sponge.

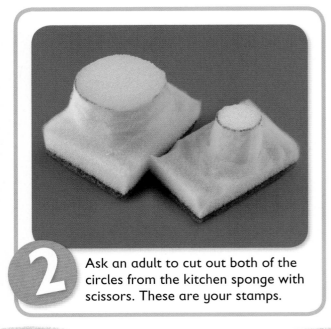

2 Ask an adult to cut out both of the circles from the kitchen sponge with scissors. These are your stamps.

3 Carefully dip the big circle stamp into some green paint and the small circle stamp into yellow paint.

4 Use the stamps to print a wavy line of green circles. Add some yellow circles for the caterpillar's feet.

5 Paint two white eyes. Use a black felt-tip pen to add a smile and two black circles inside the eyes.

6 When the paint is dry you can use the black felt-tip pen to add some details to the picture.

Bubble Cards

Try making some of these fun cards. You will need paints, card stock, paper, glue and bubble wrap.

1 You can start this project by cutting a large rectangle from a clean piece of plastic bubble wrap.

2 Brush some paint over the bubble wrap. Don't paint the edges of the wrap as this will get messy.

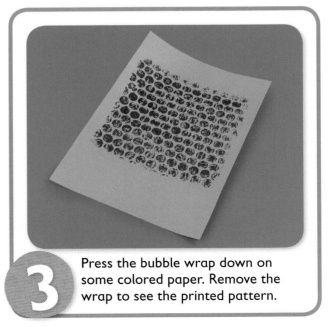

3 Press the bubble wrap down on some colored paper. Remove the wrap to see the printed pattern.

4 Practice this **technique** with different paper and paint. Try using different combinations to see what you like.

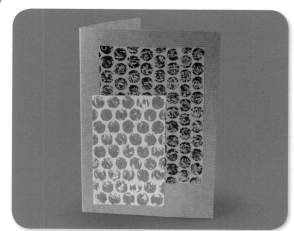

5 Now cut out different shapes from your bubble prints and use them to decorate a greeting card.

6 To finish your card, you could add some decorative paper strips or draw a border with a white pencil.

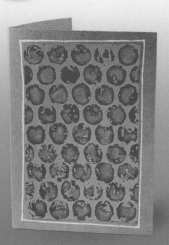

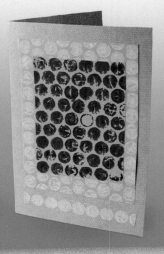

Eraser Buildings

This project is created by printing with erasers. You will also need paper, paints and a white pen.

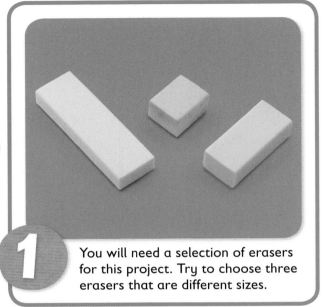

1 You will need a selection of erasers for this project. Try to choose three erasers that are different sizes.

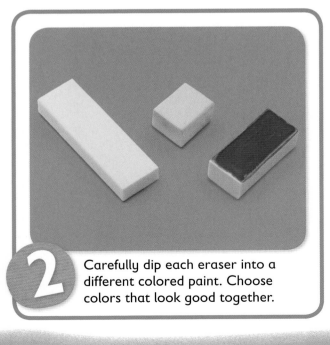

2 Carefully dip each eraser into a different colored paint. Choose colors that look good together.

3 Press the paint side of the eraser down onto some paper. Print three differently colored shapes.

4 When the first three shapes have dried, repeat this until you have lots of differently colored shapes.

5 Now take a white pen and draw windows onto each of the shapes. They now start to look like buildings.

6 To finish your city scene, you could add some birds in the sky and some vehicles on the roads.

22

Wriggly Monster

This monster is fun and messy to make. You will need string, paint, paper, and a felt-tip pen.

1 Start this project by cutting a piece of string. A piece about 1 foot (30 cm) long will be a good size to use.

2 Dip your string into some blue paint. Keep one end of the string out of the paint as this is the end you will hold.

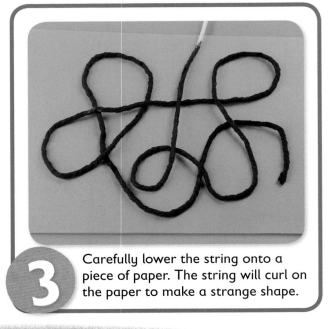

3 Carefully lower the string onto a piece of paper. The string will curl on the paper to make a strange shape.

4 Now you can lift the string off the paper. Turn the paper around to see which side looks best on top.

5 Use a felt-tip pen to draw a monster in this shape. Add eyes, feet, fingers and a mouth. Add a funny hat, too!

6 Fill some of the shapes with white paint. Why not make a friend for your monster, too?

Glossary

antennae (an-TEH-nee) Thin, rodlike organs used to feel things, located on the heads of certain animals.

materials (muh-TEER-ee-ulz) What things are made of.

outline (OWT-lyn) A line drawn around the edges of something.

patterns (PA-turnz) The way colors and shapes appear over and over again on something.

technique (tek-NEEK) A way of doing something.

Index

Further Reading

Emberley, Ed. *Ed Emberley's Complete Funprint Drawing Book*. New York: LB Kids, 2002.

Schwake, Susan. *Art Lab for Kids: 52 Creative Adventures in Drawing, Painting, Printmaking, Paper, and Mixed Media.* Beverly, MA: Quarry Books, 2012.

Websites

For web resources related to the subject of this book, go to: www.windmillbooks.com/weblinks and select this book's title.